How to Deal with
DIABETES

Kids' Health™

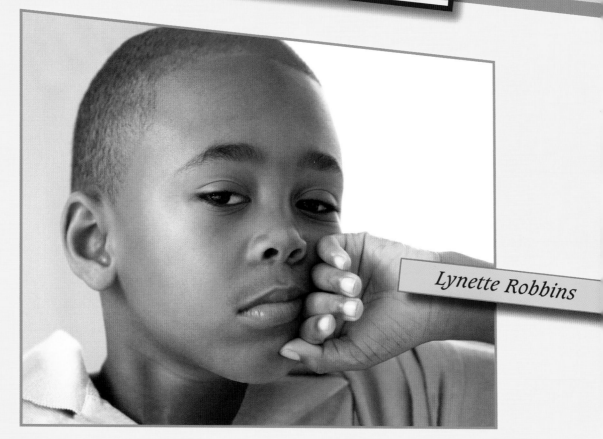

Lynette Robbins

PowerKiDS press.

New York

Published in 2010 by The Rosen Publishing Group, Inc.
29 East 21st Street, New York, NY 10010

First Edition

Editor: Joanne Randolph
Book Design: Kate Laczynski
Photo Researcher: Jessica Gerweck

Photo Credits: Cover, pp. 1, 10 Shutterstock.com; p. 4 © Richard Hutchings/Corbis; p. 6 © Visuals Unlimited/Corbis; p. 8 Altrendo Images/Getty Images; p. 12 © Laureen March/Corbis; p. 14 © Michael DeYoung/Corbis; p. 16 © Karen Kasmauski/Corbis; p. 18 © Solus-Veer/Corbis; p. 20 © Emely/zefa/Corbis.

Library of Congress Cataloging-in-Publication Data

Robbins, Lynette.
  How to deal with diabetes / Lynette Robbins. — 1st ed.
      p. cm. — (Kids' health)
  Includes index.
  ISBN 978-1-4042-8144-8 (lib. bdg.) — ISBN 978-1-4358-3425-5 (pbk.) —
ISBN 978-1-4358-3426-2 (6-pack)
  1. Diabetes in children—Juvenile literature. 2. Diabetes—Juvenile literature. I. Title.
  RJ420.D5R53 2010
  618.92'462—dc22
                                2009010467

Manufactured in the United States of America

C

4

Tired Trevor

Trevor was seven years old when he started feeling tired all the time. He felt grumpy, too. Sometimes he yelled at his little sister. Trevor was thirsty a lot. He drank a lot of water, and he went to the bathroom a lot, too. He also felt hungry most of the time. He felt as if he were always eating, but he was getting thinner and thinner.

Trevor's mother took him to the doctor. The doctor tested his blood. It was high in **glucose**. The doctor said that Trevor had an illness called diabetes. People who have diabetes cannot use the energy that is in food.

If you have diabetes, you may feel too tired to pay attention in class. If you are drinking a lot and feeling tired even when you get enough sleep, talk to your parents.

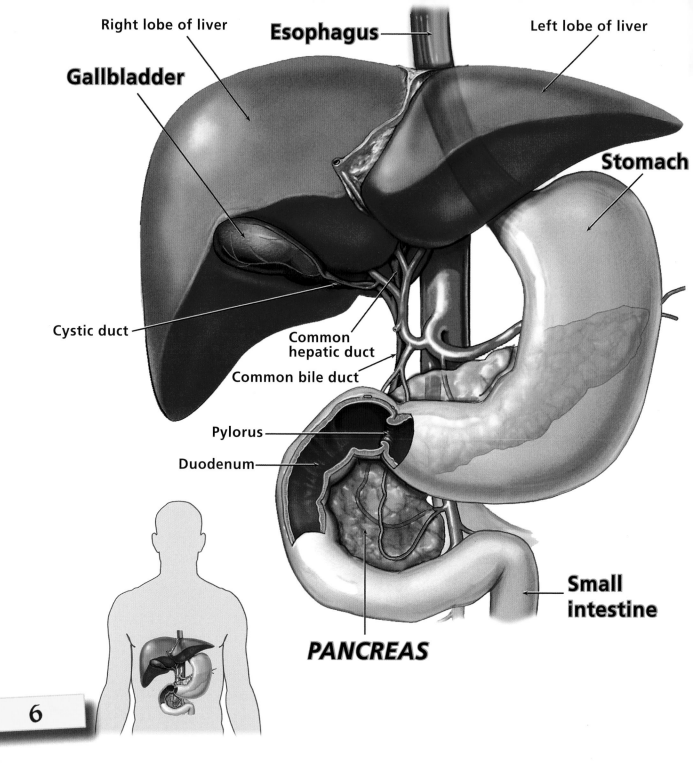

Right lobe of liver

Esophagus

Left lobe of liver

Gallbladder

Stomach

Cystic duct

Common
hepatic duct

Common bile duct

Pylorus

Duodenum

**Small
intestine**

PANCREAS

6

What Is Diabetes?

You eat food so that you have energy to do things, such as play soccer or do math problems. Whenever you eat food, your body breaks it down into a kind of sugar, called glucose. Glucose flows through your blood and into your **cells**, where it is used for energy. Glucose cannot get into your cells without **insulin**, though.

Insulin is made in a part of your body called the **pancreas**. The pancreas of a diabetic person makes very little or even no insulin. This means the person's cells cannot take in glucose to make energy. There is no cure for diabetes, but there are ways to treat it.

The pancreas is the small brown part behind the stomach and small intestine in this picture. The pancreas may be small, but it has a big job to do!

Types of Diabetes

There are two main types of diabetes, called type 1 and type 2. The pancreas of a person with type 1 diabetes does not make any insulin. Type 1 diabetes usually starts in children or young adults.

Type 2 diabetes is more common than type 1. It **develops** slowly. First, cells in the body develop insulin resistance. This means that they cannot use insulin properly. The pancreas tries to make more insulin, but it gets worn out. After a while, the pancreas can no longer make enough insulin. Older people and people who are **obese** are more at risk of developing type 2 diabetes. However, more and more young people have been getting it, too.

The number of obese children and children with diabetes is on the rise. Type 2 diabetes used to be uncommon in children, but now it is seen in more children than type 1 is.

Do I Have Diabetes?

Even though you cannot see if there is too much glucose in your blood, you can look for **symptoms** of diabetes. People who have diabetes get very thirsty and very hungry because their bodies want more energy. They eat and drink a lot, and they use the bathroom a lot. Even though they eat a lot of food, many people with diabetes lose weight instead of gaining it. They may also feel tired and **irritable**. Some people with diabetes also have trouble with their eyes.

If you have any of these symptoms, it is important to see your doctor right away! Your doctor can give you a test to see if you have diabetes.

Feeling really thirsty is often one of the first signs that you have diabetes. If you are drinking a lot and have any of the other symptoms of diabetes, tell a parent right away. 11

Eating Right

Everyone should eat a well-balanced diet. If you have diabetes, it is even more important to eat healthily. Eating a healthy diet will help keep you from getting too much glucose in your blood. To eat a healthy diet, you will have to eat few sugary snacks and eat a lot of vegetables, fruits, and whole grains.

Often, people with diabetes follow a meal plan. A doctor or **nutritionist** can work with you and your parents to make a meal plan that is just right for you! It is important to follow your meal plan so that you can stay healthy.

Making healthy choices about what you eat can go a long way toward helping you control your diabetes. Choose fruits, vegetables, and other foods that are low in sugar and fat.

Staying Active

Exercise is good for everyone, but it is especially good for people with diabetes. Exercise lowers the glucose levels in your blood. If you exercise, you may be able to eat more. You may not have to take as much insulin.

There are many ways to stay active. You can walk, play soccer, ride your bike, or swim. If you are playing a team sport, make sure your coach knows you have diabetes. It is a good idea to eat a healthy snack before you exercise. Your doctor may also ask you to test your blood sugar level before and after you exercise.

Taking a bike ride with your family is one way to get exercise. Be sure you have something sweet with you, though, in case your blood sugar drops too low.

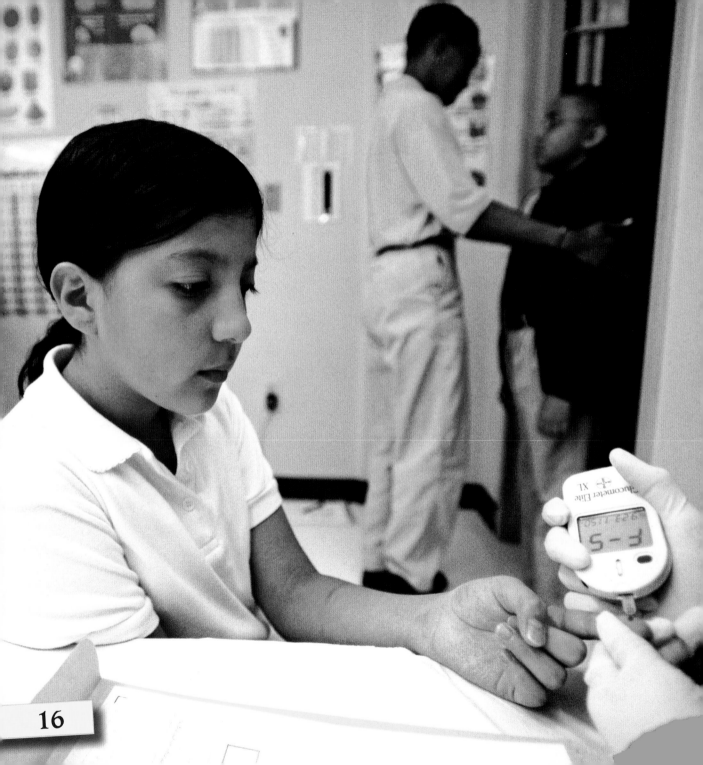

Testing Your Blood

Some people who have diabetes need to test their blood several times a day. The test tells them how much glucose is in their blood. It is important not to have too much or too little glucose in your blood.

To test your blood, you must put a drop of blood on a special test strip. The test strip is put into a small machine, called a glucose reader. The glucose reader tells you how much glucose is in your blood. If you do not have enough glucose in your blood, drinking fruit juice will help. If you have too much glucose, you may need to take extra insulin.

This girl is having her blood checked using a glucose reader. The machine tests the drop of blood on her finger and tells her whether her blood glucose is high, low, or just right.

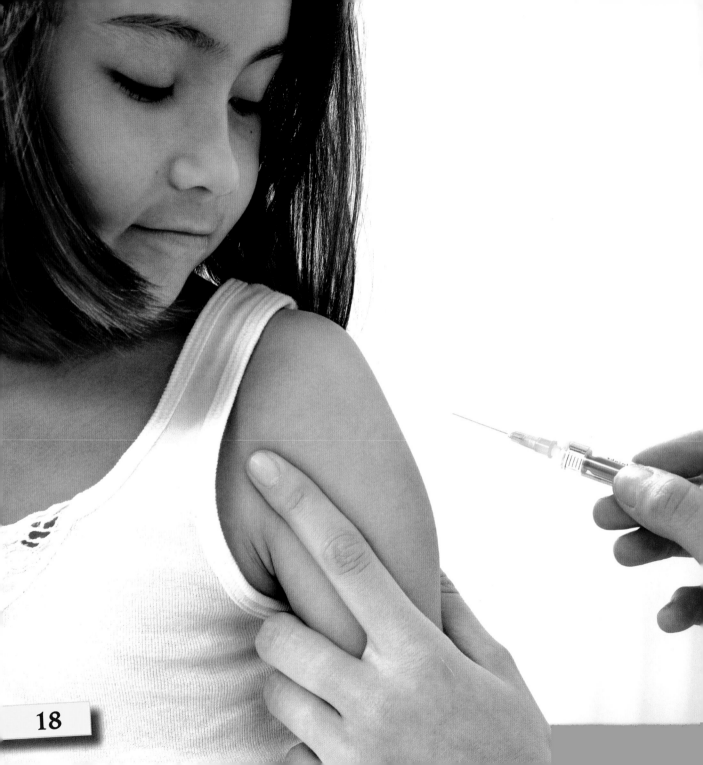

Give Me a Shot!

People who have type 1 diabetes must take insulin to help the glucose in their blood get into their cells. Most people give themselves shots of insulin. Parents or other caregivers can give young children the shots. People with diabetes may need to give themselves two, or sometimes three or four, shots of insulin each day.

Karen found out that she had diabetes when she was eight years old. At first, she disliked the insulin shots. She cried whenever she got one. After a while, she got used to them. Now Karen never cries when she gets a shot. She knows that the insulin keeps her healthy.

Insulin shots put the insulin just under the skin, not into a vein or a muscle. The drug moves from there into the blood.

Too Low

If a person with diabetes does not get enough to eat or uses too much energy, his glucose level can get too low. This is called **hypoglycemia**. A hypoglycemic person will suddenly feel sick. He may feel shaky, hot, and **confused**. The person may start having trouble seeing clearly and may behave strangely. He might even fall over or pass out.

Someone who is hypoglycemic needs sugar right away! Fruit juice, soda, or candy will work. After about 10 minutes, the person should feel better. If you have diabetes, you should carry something sweet with you at all times, just in case. However, do not eat these snacks unless you need them, since eating sugary snacks all the time is not healthy.

If you are at home when you start feeling hypoglycemic, drinking a glass of orange juice is a good way to raise your blood glucose quickly.

When a person first finds out that she has diabetes, it can be really scary. There is a lot to learn. There is also a lot you must do to stay healthy. It can take a while to learn how to follow a meal plan. It may be hard to get used to daily blood tests and insulin shots.

Luckily, there are many people who can help. Doctors, family members, **counselors**, and friends can all help you manage, or take care of, your diabetes. You do not have to let diabetes stop you from having fun or living your life. If you do a good job taking care of yourself, you can keep your body healthy and strong!

GLOSSARY

cells (SELZ) The basic units, or pieces, of living things.

confused (kun-FYOOZD) Mixed up.

counselors (KOWN-seh-lerz) People who talk with people about their feelings and problems and who give advice.

develops (dih-VEH-lups) Grows or happens over time.

exercise (EK-ser-syz) Moving one's body to get or stay fit.

glucose (GLOO-kohs) The sugar that the body uses for energy, or the power to do things.

hypoglycemia (hy-poh-gly-SEE-mee-uh) A sickness in which people do not have enough sugar in their blood.

insulin (IN-suh-lin) Matter made by the pancreas that is needed for the use of sugar and starch in one's body.

irritable (IR-uh-tuh-bel) Easily annoyed.

nutritionist (noo-TRIH-shuh-nist) A person who teaches others about healthy eating.

obese (oh-BEES) Very overweight.

pancreas (PANG-kree-us) A part inside the body that makes insulin.

symptoms (SIMP-tumz) Signs that show someone is sick.

INDEX

WEB SITES

Due to the changing nature of Internet links, PowerKids Press has developed an online list of Web sites related to the subject of this book. This site is updated regularly. Please use this link to access the list: www.powerkidslinks.com/heal/diabetes/